Geometry of the Od

Geometry of the Odd

Stan Rogal

Wolsak and Wynn . Toronto

© Stan Rogal, 1999

All rights reserved. No part of this book may be reproduced or transmitted in any form, by any means, electronic or mechanical, without permission in writing from the publisher, except by a reviewer who may quote brief passages in a review. In case of photocopying or other reprographic copying, a licence is required from CANCOPY (Canadian Copyright Licensing Agency), One Yonge Street, Suite 1900, Toronto, ON, CANADA M5E 1E5.

Typeset in Garamond, printed in Canada by
The Coach House Printing Company, Toronto.

Front cover art:: Jacquie Jacobs
Cover design: Stan Bevington
Author's photograph: Berge Arabian / Contrast

The author wishes to thank the following magazines & editors for publishing many of the poems: *Ink* (ON), *Jones Av* (ON), *Waking Ordeals* (ON), *Fiddlehead* (NB), *Stuff* (ON), *Acta Victoriana* (ON), *Kairos* (ON), *Queen St. Quarterly* (ON), *Afterthoughts* (ON), plus the anthology *Written In The Skin* (ON). He also thanks the Canada Council for awarding a "B" grant to this project. Thanks, as well, to those who recommended grants through the Ontario Arts Council's "Writers Reserve Program" and also CANCOPY and the Public Lending Rights Commission. Your support was not only welcome, but necessary.

The publishers gratefully acknowledge the support of the Canada Council for the Arts for our publishing program.

Wolsak and Wynn Publishers Ltd.
Post Office Box 316
Don Mills, Ontario, Canada M3C 2S7

Canadian Cataloguing in Publication Data

Rogal, Stan, 1950-
  Geometry of the Odd

Poems.
ISBN 0-919897-63-0
I. Title.
PS8585,O391G46 1999   C811',54   C99-930856-4
PR9199.3.R63G46 1999

*This book is dedicated to Jacquie,
for her love, humour & energy. Awed in an odd world.*

Where chaos begins classical science stops — James Gleick

The more you understand an age, the more convinced you become that the images a given poet used and which you thought his own were taken almost unchanged from another poet ... poets are more concerned with arranging images than with creating them. Images are given to poets; the ability to remember them is far more important than the ability to create them. By "works of art" in the narrow sense, we mean works created by special techniques designed to make the works as obviously artistic as possible.

— Viktor Shklovsky

CONTENTS

Introduction   9

Geometry of the odd   10
Alchemical: The first   12
Familiar   14
Into the wood   15
Idolatries   16
Psalm XXII: Reprisal   17
Inside out   18
It was suddenly as if   20
Sub Rosa   21
She conceives   23
Alchemical: The second   24
Kind of blue: An elegy   26
Storm front   28
Insomnious   30
The St. Louis Sporting News, blues   31
The corruption   33
Alchemical: The third   34
Tango   35
Outlaws   37
Lament   38
The Look   39
Legend   41
The Common Sense Revolution   42
Settled   44
Talk, talk   45
Body Politic   46
Alchemical: The fourth   47
Stuck   48
Sonata form: Exposition   50
Sonata form: Development   52
Sonata form: Recapitulation   54
Breaking the Waves: The Poem   56
Eclogue   58
Hale-Bopp & the 39   61
Rosemary   64
The scream   66
Cowboy dreams   68

For what it's worth   69
Dictionary   71
Beauty   72
Alchemical: The fifth   73
St Elmo's Fire   76
The big smoke   77
Wish you were here   79
Blue moon   81
Codes   82
Ghosts   83
Fortune   84
The Cassandra complex   85
Pop figure   86

INTRODUCTION

I must admit that I am, indeed, pleased and honoured to be summoned, so to speak, from the other side by Mr. Rogal to offer a few words regarding his manuscript. I had wondered whether any of us — the metaphysical poets — would be remembered at all, except possibly as a curious footnote, myself especially, and here it is, 300 years later. In truth, it is surprising that anyone is writing poetry at all anymore, given that the endeavour is particularly unrewarding in most societies. That being said (and aside), I would like to welcome Mr. Rogal among our group, for better or for worse.

His work is rife with arresting and original images and conceits (showing a preoccupation between macrocosm and microcosm), wit, ingenuity, dextrous use of colloquial speech, considerable flexibility of rhythm and metre, complex themes (both sacred and profane — which seem to come down to the same brief matter for him), a liking for paradox and dialectical argument, a direct manner, a caustic humour, a keenly felt awareness of mortality, and a distinguished capacity for elliptical thought and tersely compact expression. But for all of Mr. Rogal's intellectual robustness, he is also capable of refined delicacy, gracefulness and deep feeling; passion as well as wit.

This, for what it's worth and for whomsoever is interested and listening. A heartfelt and fond adieu.

Your servant, Andrew Marvell
(1621-1678)

GEOMETRY OF THE ODD

> *I don't know whether to kill myself or go bowling.*
> — Judith Fitzgerald

Stuck in a surround of woods. What could be
Anywhere else on this flat earth. But isn't. Is
Here. A place where everything begins & ends
  in middles
    strikes as nowhere to a dead-beat heart.
For sake of a single disremembered cup
I wander missing & never-never-to-return.
No Atlas me. A last. A salt. A slat
Nailed across a pane from which
No face. No figure. No faint recollection.
Even allowing the possibility
I don't miss something good if I come upon it
Won't vanquish the fact.
A simply drawn breath
Terrifies
In its ability to stretch a lung
    past the limits of a tennis court.

    What is within is without & vice versa.

The fear that issues from a land
    that calls on ice to produce heat
        even as it freezes
    remains
A mystery. Or:
        how the patterns of earthquakes also govern the
        distribution of incomes in a free-market economy
        fuels the 2nd Law of Thermodynamics
        & slides a state toward increasing disorder.
Final cause, remarks: the earth is what it is
    so that humanity can do what it does.
Hardly settling
The expression of our failure
To orient ourselves in a physical universe has us
Pinning butterfly wings to the backs of mountains
Only to see them flutter once & vanish.

Look up! Trees have stars in their hair & the spines
   of hanged men
      slowly coil toward the upper branches.
Within the frame of this raptured blue light
The same shots repeat over & over again
From every angle & at every speed.
Clearly, the quarterback's ankle snaps.
Clearly, the putt drops from sixty feet.
Clearly, the bullet worms its way through the skull
   & out the other side.
There is a certain amount of suggestiveness that is
(Clearly)
Necessary.
Now imagine a human being scaled up twice its size
& you imagine a structure whose bones collapse
   under its own weight.

Who cannot not remain foreign among
With bare pubes, shaggy tits & an unerring eye
For the obvious, cries:
         "We are all of us robust, strange &
         Doomed."
Suffer the little children? The little children.
They do. Suffer. Whereas I wouldn't normal be caught
Dead. Yet, a quest improves upon acquaintance (they say)
& figures
         Now that I'm here, I'm here.
         I'd misrecognize me anywhere.

ALCHEMICAL: THE FIRST

I have wet lips & know the art of losing
old conscience in the depths of a bed.
— Charles Baudelaire

Odd & in love at worst, at best
Fomenting in the fractious teeth of it
Who long for a purely vagrant path are nicked as
Criminal
    between heart-of-hearts with minds bent to no good
    listening.
Listen.
At base, facts never explain anything without
Fantasy to intercourse
Blood runs cold & the strict sun directly
Withers.
Given this frame
How can we not not love?
Whether in dreams, in bars or huddled in darkness
The potential to spark
Marks any door a window offering
Endless
Flights
Of stars.

Hung up by most improper woods
Will you come to me
Configures incubus & succubus aroused
At the sight of leaded lids now soon to be
Laid to rest.
Miss libidinal & how
Poetry
    flowers out of joint.
Half-hearted belief thirst for variety
Invariably leads to bloodshed
Must also half-concur confinement binds together
Combinations wanting colour, mainly: gold.
Whereas to attempt the invisible is to need
The courage of an alien
A promise, kiss or ring are relics signifying
Nothing

We know
Familiarity breeds indifference
& flow shifting from smooth to turbulent
Breaks all polite observations.
As well, what rhymes with reason is
Alas & alack
Stood up waiting at the altar
Without a prayer.

The maligned hand (meanwhile) being proffered
By lovers & fools alike
Fingers the odyssey in a land plagued
    with hoary hags & demons.
It is precisely here, along some fatal descent
    an innocent mole
        breaks a trail
           & bodies seek heat
    for the sheer
Adventure.
No regrets, coyote.
Faith in the premise that
    every dream is a repressed burning
With a lipstick
Sets her mouth
A blaze.

FAMILIAR

she looks like someone
her face
looking like
& yet   somehow
not the face
but
otherwise, like,
some passing
(maybe)
thing
        perhaps
a motion
you
recall

INTO THE WOOD

Heart like a wheel is such distant country.
Nothing with no mind to stop it
Can. Nor would want to.
As a map laid out flat as anything does not move us.
But a mountain
Is a different story.
Or a river. Or a tree.
Can you hear that lonesome whippoorwill?
Hear it. Its voice frail in the timbered wood.
Caught up, like they say.
Like they'd wish to be.
Unlike the noise we call
Language
Will never echo
So strange.
A motion.

IDOLATRIES

Pinned to this rough sheet the map unrolls backwards.
No direction but where they've been
& conscience a cloaked wood staked deep
    to the very heart of it.

Woods cannot open another's mind.
The way those big trees seem to somehow just amaze
Is not the duty of a tree
    or any other growth.

Unprepared for such emptiness they push woods
All their worth. Nimby armed against the unk-unks
Makes patriotism a brand
    burnt into the brains of the dead.

How despair amid such beauty? Amid such calm? Easy.
Saddled by a country where a wild voice is broke by custom
The demand for unconditional love
    binds every heart to earth.

Nature as a source of oracles is not the idiocy.
The idiocy is belief in God's goodness & omnipotence
In the face of so much evil.
To escape one's powerlessness by destroying the world
Frames God-masquerading-as-God
Far outside the golden gates
This is Hell
Using gasoline & a match
    to scrape the ashes from his teeth.

PSALM XXII: REPRISAL
My God, why hast thou forsaken me?

Not starting over again but similar.
The decision not to amounting to the same
Lack
Nature
against its will tangles root for root producing
    beauty
        whereas a mind
Misshapes.
Let's figure out. Where we stand is where we fall
& a hero is no longer.
Hardware runs without permission at this crossing
While software suffers the habits of age.
"Man is a huddle of need," reflected John,
    barely looking before he leaped.
The new geometry is (as well) rough, not rounded.
Like your flesh turns sudden
Foreign
& a voice once inclined to soothe
Now tumbles violation.
Whether fluttered wings, pulsive moons or beaten hearts
At a point of crisis small changes register out of proportion
Rendering manifest
    ghostly forms in motion
    lie
    behind the matter.
Hunger begun to feed upon itself & every particle
    seeking an opposite with which to end.
Not having killed myself for seeming centuries echoes:
There is a hole within this frame
A parting
        I am poured out like water.
        All my bones are out of joint.

INSIDE OUT

Rainy afternoon with fog & sparrows.
Whether in or out of frame
this is the act
observation brings to play.
As your reflection is never misplaced
but remains somehow oddly a part.
Oddly. The way some seeming *insignificant*
can make you
    just break down & cry.
Like, a few crumbs scattered on the sill
or the world's mad rush past your window
or a slight shift in design
    causes patterns of excitation
        wave & particle, particle & wave
    migrating south to
no comfort; no heat.
Saul's blind bellowing aside,
almost no one dies of heartbreak
anymore
whereas the accident of a small bird
crashing against the glass
invites
distortion.
On the spot, there is a funeral.
It's pretty nice.
It kind of blows & whistles in the breeze.
You are almost disproportionately happy
in your grief.
Then, for whatever no good reason, you think:
    "The process of creation ties in with
    the dismemberment of the body."
& so on.
Then just as suddenly, you think:
    "A chain of events can have a point of
    crisis that could magnify small changes."
& so on.

Then, you think:
> "The pressure exerted by a dominant poetics
> has always shaped the art of lesser minds."
& so on.
Then, you think:
> "You don't know what love is until
> you've had the blues."
& so on, & so forth, & etcetera ...
Everything contained in the face of it
flashes flesh & feathers, hands & claws
until you are nothing but an outline.
A window frame offering a view of landscape.
Or the landscape itself.
The line loosing all hold on separation
recollects:

Some things far away
get close before you know it.

IT WAS SUDDENLY AS IF

"Ah" she said &
"Ah"
       her head
       tilted
that way
away, she said: "Ah"
&
  nothing more
the head
       tilted
"Ah" she said
finally
& "Ah" I said
the head
       tilted
away
"Ah" we said
finally
& "Ah"
    & "Ah"
       & "Ah"

SUB ROSA

Unconditional imperative provides a sorry tense.
Just as love
    bearing a hard right
        then riding off into the sunset
    remains
incomplete
stuck neither above nor below
this worn line
flames each direction
erotic & pure.
Weather
    pressed between milky sheets
    or pressed between the bloody petals of the rose
    is still
weather
yet, ill-at-ease with the suggestion

              we create the world

at the moment of weakness
things shift from smooth to turbulent
    then back again.
To what no good end?
Long broke of the need to raise the hem
of the unknown
the wish to exist
in two places simultaneously
just about
    impossible.
Just about. Though not ½ so much as this desire
failing
    to land on one proper heart or an other.
Heat no simple atom could endure without splitting
intends to live happy-ever-after
    & no thought toward a random motion
        set to cut the legs out from under.

Like, the primitive action
of undoing the bolts, locks & latches
to facilitate birth
forgets
the process of creation
ties in
   with the dismemberment of the body.
What chance to wax European when sub rosa
roughly translates
a lack
in this provincial tongue?

Given a land ruled by sorcery
warp & woof ravel in the after-glow, contending:
   the act of playing the game
   has a way of changing the rules.
A far cry from where things stand.
Unallowing a flaw in the fabric
to catch a fit glimpse
the mind's attempt to get at the heart
lacks all control
pushing love to the limit of no limit
& ending
   tangled in the weave.

for Siv Cedering Fox
SHE CONCEIVES

    Poems
    children & a husband
    balances each
    they share
    fingertips, hair
    her kissing lips
    the close O of breasts
    &
        distance

    precise &
    uncompromising
    she relegates
    what, when, who
    enters her cunt
    leaves it
    transforms it
    is transformed
    by it

    O creative O
    she dis/covers
    passageways
    linking
    her self
    to
    the world

ALCHEMICAL: THE SECOND
> *We are not free & the heavens can still fall upon our heads.*
> — Antonin Artaud

Strangest thing happen.
Caught myself thinking again. Too late.
Been deep in the sauce three long weeks
& see it taking.
The mind tricks
    with anthropological fascination.
Owning up
a sensitive dependence on initial condition
I am awed
    by the spitting image.
For a start, my self-portrait
recognized
    doesn't always terrify.
Or the brainpan cast without a hint of gold
goes largely unregistered.
Meanwhile, what occurs outside this bottled scape
would cause a cat to scream.
Whether the migratory habits of glaciers
or the insinuating vapours of combustive lizards
a moving object tends to keep moving
& location ceases to exist.
I mean:
        If every cubic centimetre of empty space
        contains more energy than the total energy
        of all matter in the universe ...
Where does that leave me?
How much identity is sufficient?
Stigmata aside
Hitler's teeth rattling the chain
is little difference.
Held fast to nothing save a skull & cross
    bones
        slip untouched between the cracks.
Who extols the benefits of booze
permits existence in the world's
fabrication.

here is the proper use of what works to get along

Mainly, the maker dead & gone, I am damned.
Sure with the task of carving myself from stone
in order to advance.
Yet, why struggle to be a man when you can be
a success?
Despite appearances (they say)
    we are beings without borders; not things,
        but relatively independent subtotalities.
I vomit in the hole.
Clausius's dogged 2nd Law licks its chops
& pulls a grave across my face.
Reasons enough, at times, to consider.
A poisoned apple.
A bullet through the brain.
Leave the old grey mass, heavied, to dream in its cave.
Become no less an animal than a god, now.
Or a single grain of sand.
Cats mew, dogs bark, humans
(all too frequent)
Flag.

*Rudolf Clausius formulated the 2nd Law of Thermodynamics

KIND OF BLUE: AN ELEGY

Down with the miseries & miles blown cool across the wire.
What comes to bear along a line. Though, not so much a line
  as waves. Pattern. The blues.
Is not unhappiness but a feel for.
Rhythms & modes allowing relations between.
Different planes of reality.
Forms forming & reforming. Things (said Jack)
  do not connect; they correspond.
Mood being at least as sublime as sense
  a split tongue or a split lip perform the same
Mutilated
Music.
Amid the swamp of everyday rides in
A variation on a theme:

Are we sick of angels, yet?

I am. Sick. Am. No angel.
Rather, sporting black mustachio & packing heat
Fashion the air both robust & strange.
When I come from was a time.
Now way past when I would make a Jane
  with a six-pack of Moody Blue & a few narrow lines.
Everyone over-sensitive praying
  sex, drugs & alcohol to occur as metaphor, only,
Are disturbed.
Are unable to pick up on a solo beat & realize
    dissipation bleeds
    a complex system of conflicting motions
    which eventually bring the behaviour of
    many dimensions down to one.

Knowing I'm really in a vein if I can direct myself.
The more the focus, the more the melody breaks.
As turning it over in my head.
Her slowly removing her coat.
Trying her best not to look sensual.

You can leave your hat on ... you can leave your hat on ...
 you can leave your hat on ...

As turning her over in the bed.
Visualizing the shape one can appreciate the system.
The hook. The line. The phrase that catches. The look.
That kills.
As nature doing a thing against its will.
Out of the tangle emerges beauty.

What ends the sentimental lyric?
Not bitterness, but boredom, pal.
Questions the use of such thin music
 that ribbons past the rocks
  then disappears over the edge without a trace.

Will you pleasure me with your mouth?
You did. Do. Entered & entering to no fixed destination.
The angels (meantime) remain. Sorely absent.
Their hearts & genitalia packed in goose-down.
Not by your own hand, not that, but, the *body*
Hung by a spike in time of plague
Offered up as an open invitation, miles,
To the blues
Taken.

STORM FRONT
To the pure all things are pure.

What's lived is the devil.
What's livid is something meaner
Meaning
Weather
    argued ontologically or by faith
    cannot escape the influence
God's
(Or an other One's)
Great double standard
    lights up the dance floor with furious rumour.
Weather
    reddish; enraged; discoloured by bruising
    is not so
    necessarily
Weather
God's dog or dog's god
Air charges amid the gnash & snarl.
Here marks the mysterious point
    when an orderly system turns chaotic.

So, tell me – how is life in the temperate zone? Temperate? Comfortable? Bearable? Boring? What forked mercurial makes the tongue wag in such an idyll heaven?

Thrown hard upon this *xy axis* configure
Love's strict platitude crossed over & hung to dry
Through small, uncontrollable circumstance.
Evidence
An innocent two-step, say, or waltz
Become sudden languorous.
Become sudden driven by hips gone soft in the middle.
Become sudden bodies pressured at the joint.
Become sudden barely keeping time, but, making time
To the insistent pulse & beat.
Become sudden moment of weakness, fatal arrow or strange
Attractor
    tearing the flesh in sudden myriad mad direction.

Become sudden weather causing
Shifts in temperature
   to re-pattern atmospheric conditions
     where sudden rise & fall makes all the difference.
As a storm front closing in.
As Sam Jaffe flush for a nickel's worth
Of a young girl's tarantella
Gets iced by the cops.

How long were you out there, watching? Long enough, pal.

Call it bad timing.
Call it slippery footage; endless loop.
Action triggered by a minimum image sets the hounds loose,
    their eyes fired by a pregnant moon;
       their teeth lurid with the telling blood of entrails.
Honey in the jawbone won't cut it.
Not an appeal to restless nature.
Nor, even, the booze.

        I don't drinks no more. 'Course,
        I don't drinks no less, neither.

The air conditioner hums.
The electric blanket works like a charm.
Destiny takes its turbulent course &
A man
Has been known to drown
In less than half an inch of
(Otherwise) friendly
Fire.

INSOMNIOUS

Not a journey but a concurrence.
Unlike the awed sea cradling the moon on its back.
Or the dream dreaming itself out of control, but, otherly.
Fallen.
Knowing the dangers yet feeling it had to go ahead.
Any way. Split in two.
Whether of its own accord or through an other
Necessary
Heat
This
Is the heart of it. Aware
    that even surfaces in contact do not touch everywhere
    makes for some deep & maculate.
Conception? Hardly.
A transfiguration of self to self-same
Conduct
Along a path both beat & beaten.
The heart, again, for all the matter, existing, outside.
As those three positions allowed for a man
        in a woman's life: husband, lover, friend.
Are taken (somehow) circumstantial.
Evidence, this:
        Madness
        being the climactic phase
        of one's dissolution with the world
        affords some strange &
        attractive
Here.
Now.
At base, the rational feeds upon the irrational
& against the innocent stars & remorseless seas
A heading, of sorts, bears remarking.
The thing, stripped of any vagrant sign, awakes.
Digs in. Takes hold.

THE ST. LOUIS SPORTING NEWS, BLUES

Weather
Strung out along a bass line
or gone bats up some tropic stream.
Any game called on account'a
rain
forests the trebled heart
& where the riff breaks
    blues
        pound oddly formed rhythms.
What might seem the furthest word
from manicured diamonds
fits hand-in-glove for a trip
fuelled by cool chops, hot licks &
    attraction
        for the torrid zone.

Here exists such wild pitch that drives spectators
native:
    hum now, hum now, hum now, baby ...

Never once allowed to ignore or forget
players stretched beyond the limits of their legs
are easy pickings.
Either beat off the bag, going for two,
or rounding third with an eye for home
get caught short by a one-hopper
drilled deep from right.
Shagging flies in a country that, normal, refuses flies
beside every other buzzy jam
Poetry (as well) thrown high & inside
fails to catch the corner
all ways.

A place where sidemen signal junk
& trees versed in proper paper product
fall, as jazz falls to the timbered grace
of a four-balled trumpeter
Goose or Satchmo blowing lead in a bottomed-out
seventh half-note:
   score tied, bases full, two gone, end of nine
Sympathy sounds nowhere with no sharp ear to close
& give relief. Simply, left stranded on the mound
gaze up from the jungled mix
envision
diamonds' star-struck fire
burn indelible light
upon this dim
teeming
field.

THE CORRUPTION

> *It is by being 'natural' that one recovers from
> one's unnaturalness, from one's spirituality.*
> —Friedrich Nietzsche

What human touch disfigures
   the eye can merely guess at.
Even given the need for flaws
Or the malice of the inanimate object
Fails to cut it.
Like, the sound you take to be an ocean
Rolls sudden silent in the parched night.
A salt smell lingers on the tongue tip, but,
   the ocean, for all its baffled history
      of white whales & drowned men
   can never begin to swell
Outside itself.
Unlike desire for a body held against you
Bones
No idolatry can hope to exhume
   long to thrill & crash beneath your flesh.
Who sacrifices accuracy for insight
Misrecognizes
Vision
   is what the eye falls hard upon. Simply:

   the act of perception is an act of creation.

Complicated with the taste of an other who
Says, "Men get erect, women bloom"
Makes the attempt to slip
Passion between the legs of love
A corruption.
How flow shifts from smooth to turbulent
Breaks all rules.
Here exists the random order, *heaven knows.*
At this impasse, simple shapes become inhuman
& a single memory haunts
   the scent of every pillow:
        the dream dreaming itself out of control.

ALCHEMICAL: THE THIRD

Stand confused in the clearing, eh?
No longer secure "in a dark wood
      where the straight way was lost."
Infernal Dante gone to hell in this circumstance
Unable to strike the slightest match.
Rita Hayworth or the Duke, let's say, standing there.
Standing there sorely amazed. Without exception
Bent
    toward this shifting transitory
        their jaws hung, the eyes of Texas hard upon.
Yucca flats or every other promised land
Given over to heat & a mushrooming black cloud.
Here is death in life & life in death
That ravages an entire crew – phoney Huns
    as subject as anybody to which way the wind blows
        now never to return except as grave image
    on a film run ragged with myriad insistent
Teeth.
How live deliberately
Confronted with one's own
Mortality?
Those voices that howl in the wilderness draw a blank.
The wheels fall abruptly by the way for no good reason.
Only know:
                Conqueror is a crab
                forsaking any golden Beatrice
                to regenerate
                this played-out odyssey.

TANGO

It's a weepy afternoon for all that.
For all that foolin' around. No foolin' –
Whether
    we love or not fails to alter circumstance.
Not those things that rise in flame then close in frost
Nor the very fact of it.
Snowflakes fingerprint the window.
The city digs in for another four months of winter.
The thermometer's dropt & dropping still.
Still, in this room, smouldering between the remains
    of omelettes & the reek of coffeed sex
        Piazzola grinds out a fevered *Milonga Picaresque*.
A woman's blonde figure cuts the dark air, saying,
    she awoke in the night with a snore in her nose
        roaming her pillow like some small rough beast.
Her name is Maria or Sonja or Eva.
She dances bare-assed & has never been to
Buenos Aires.
I sit naked myself, thinking,
Nowhere
    has there ever been an icy room
        with a window toward a sultry beach
            & a dark woman wounding the blonde air with
Requiems.
I may be wrong. Fantasy & fact intermingle in the heat.
Temperature heads for the temperature of the room
& velocity heads for zero.
Unlike the woman (variously called Brigit or Ingrid or Liv)
Who wields her arms like knives.
'Time, here, is circular,' she says.
That, & that breasts are funny things. When hers grew,
    her feet disappeared.
Piazzola leans hot & heavy into *Tango Apasionado*.
I lean a nail against the passive glass.
'The final snowflake,' I say, 'records the history
    of all the changing weather conditions
It has experienced along the way.'
The woman (whose name is a ruin outside this space)
Breathes the flake into a boiling tear.

'I'm cold,' she says, setting her nipples ablaze,
'& the neighbours are getting turned on.'
Me too, her suddenly rude as a clam.
Her hand upon my member
Realizes
    the immediacy of her tactile response
        to the drama of the moment.
Come with a price, yes, but,
Whether
    animal attraction, potential to spark
        or desire to kiss until the lips bleed
At each step
Complication
Gains rewards.
Piazzola laying down his bandoneon ends the *Cyclical Night*.
Here, for a time, contains a manageable form of the
Terrifying.
The window rages in a choke of fire & ash.
Beyond,
    the bleak world chatters,
        picks up its dying
Lament.

OUTLAWS

Hostile to this horizontal/vertical plain
Diagonals are somehow suspect
Seeming (almost) to suggest
    some particular real object or other.
A figure, for instance, all erections & disasters
    slumped in a doorway, smoking, using a
        struck match to pick the dandruff from his teeth.
In truth, not hard to look at, yet, hardly
A fit role model.
Everything come from promise, now laid to waste
Forgets
Man is what he leaves behind:
        bones, ashes or the butt-ends of cigarettes
        accounting equal weight.
Who is known *strictly* for being known
    presents the authentic fake, leaned back
        & lighting up a Lucky.
What bright-eyed & bushy-tailed could hope
Such brilliant
Glory?
Strange. Stranger. This worship of the unreal
    that frees us from responsibility
        & keeps us on our knees.
Sure as hell, atoms tend to disintegration:
        the Marlboro man or every other idol
        Dead
        Died
        Headed
                for the hills.

LAMENT

What bigger waste of time than this is.
On slippery footing from the gun
Gets bushwacked at every undertaking.
How dress a corpse with such infinitely small
Vocabulary?
At bottom, where the prize is no bottom
Simply space
    & the faint glow of what may or may not be stars
Remains the fear.
To do anything except sit with the hands folded, yet,
For all its heartfelt
At the ragged edges of the world men rot
Impaled on barbed wire fencing.
No amount of poetry
    transforms these wounds to roses.
No amount of poetry
Ever
Can.

THE LOOK

> *Give me chastity & continency, but not yet.*
> — St. Augustine

She has that look about her that
makes you want to
but you don't
because
you've been through that look
before.

Right?

Beyond this empty ring
Comes a point where the heart matters.
Being on the whole busted or otherwise on the mend
Lines of least resistance multiply
   & all patterns reduce to a single system
      of generating forces.
Even misrecognizing the critical trace of fire
   surging in the blood
Cannot escape.
From whatever distance sparks touch off.
Whether authentic fake or the real McCoy
Flow desires to realize itself
   & the available world serves as
      common ground for such structural coupling.
Never minding armed & curious
   at the bell, mouths salivate & the trunks drop.
Who doesn't figure the mating call
   of the giant west coast clam misses the
Joke.
Or asked to do the Jelly roll smiles confused
But ends rolling in the hay just the same.
Unaware how the irrational feeds the rational
   & never once caring, admits,
      we do crazy things when we're wounded.

Given the topologically perverse habits of strange
Attractors
Adopts the intentional stance:
    things occur when we are ready for them to occur.
Love grows fur in the oddest places.
If something can happen, it will.

LEGEND

Here is the country side. Staggered
Flat or rolling. Spun with thick grasses or
    spiked with wildflowers & tall stands of timber.
Big & bold as anything you can't imagine
Those mountains. That river. The fact of
    a few fallen inches of snow covering the treetops.
What is common called a landscape.
Yet, from the awed sea arises the proposition:
       What grape, to keep its place in the
       sun, taught our ancestors to make wine?
In deed
Empty
As the pilgrims' false persuasion
   about the source of oracles
      or pygmies shooting arrows at the eclipsing moon.
Adulterate nature offers such easy scape
For raptured spirits & similar low ghosts
   set to save their mortal souls
Whereas
What never took it so much to heart
Simply, to make the stone stony
Bows beneath the weight
   & is nailed at every crossing.

THE COMMON SENSE REVOLUTION

Nowhere close to angels
They
   hover above the masses like playful school chums
      slapping shoulders & nudging ribs while
   reciting the riot act.
Which begs the question:
   what's so progressive about conservatives?
Who sport dull, *Age-of-Electric* hype
   to a populace grown sick with nuclear bombast.
Who campaign a lame procession of faulty facts & figures
   while the real numbers parade
      to no good advantage below.
Who require the blood of innocents to fuel the guts
   of an economic system long gone jaded & obsolete.

Such are the limits of a common sense revolution
That has its mind stuck on reverse.
The wheels seize & the machinery lurches
Out of control
   crushing everything deemed too weak, too slow,
      or too sick to catch the new blue wave.
As if the poor & middle class share sole responsibility
Whereas any fool can figure
   money rises to the top then sits thick & heavy
      till it curdles.
Proof positive that the only trickle-down effect is
   disease & a bad taste in the mouth.
Here is the result of misplaced democracy
That has the empowered few speak for the affluent fewer
   while the many are laid to waste
      for sake of a trumped-up budget.
It's come to this.
The Ivory Tower has re-located to Bay Street.
Today's true artists are spin doctors & bean counters
   sporting designer cell-phones & claiming
      to understand the needs of the general public.

Still, they hover, only rising further above the masses.
Still, nowhere closer to angels, they spread their wings
    & it is not to embrace but to suffocate.
If this is common sense it is indeed a revolution.
Clocks turn backward.
The Dark Ages are upon us.

SETTLED

> *I guess every port of refuge has its price*
> – the Eagles

What excites a question. What does?
Seeking to secure that edge
    between the tolerable & the
Terror
Simply
Begs a life lost beneath the cushions.
Or who surrenders the self to a role model
Bottoms out, finally, left holding the bag.
Nothing more real than nothing
Provides the promise
Forever
       what is above is like what is below
       what is below is like what is above
At this base level quantity becomes quality
As the devil we know contrives
    sarcophagi within sarcophagi
        toward some mean end.
Cramped in this arena each familiar object
Puts on its ugly face
& everything shiny, sweet-smelling & mostly useless
    keeps any fervent stranger
        cooling their heels outside the door.
Where a forward step would explode all thought
In the last analysis
A lifetime spent in tears makes for some cheap & empty
Melodramatic.
What excites a question. What does?
Beyond the normal everyday
    of wandering shades & phantoms
The fear
Have the faithful departed? The faithful.
Never do.

TALK, TALK

I will affect you slowly.
Like the language of oysters
    persuading pearls from sand.
Or not.
Progress stepped up
    by mutual strange attraction
        eliminates polite preliminaries.
What call to intercourse
Blushes
Attractive
As the body's
Aural hum?
Whether electric, chemical or magnetic
Jumps the gun. Sparks
    a chain reaction, blood to bone to skin
        reducing other utterance
Meaningless.
At moment of weakness
An orderly system turns chaotic.
The tongue flickers & the teeth & lips
Melt to
Fleshy pleasures.
The orgasm
Lingering
    within its pink shell
Stirs
At the slightest irritant
Pearls.

BODY POLITIC

Wind-chill factor & definite serious drift
Delineate the party limits.
An architecture of crystalline geometry
Falling into forms
As if rank columns could substitute a heart.
Flush with the usual Victorian enchantment with statistics
Configures an endless reproduction of fixed image.
Budgets, deficits or sundry further illusaries
designed to support
    the duty-free zone of anonymous affluence
        toward the bitter business of annihilation.
Who own zero tolerance for undiminishing uncertainty
    plunge straight
        for bottom lines of lowest common denominator.
What boils down to self-interest
Fails to account
    the long division
        separating have from have not.
Since Plato's Republic no such categorical
Makes so imperative
Actions inconsiderate of result
Where desire for uniform structure turns its back
& it is not chaos but order that breeds
Horror.
From the bleating mouths of woolly-headed politicians
Snow flies & one flake piles another in a succession
    of bricks, walls & towers
        arranged to set a thinning band.
How weather the storm given such cold rule?
Being barely alive in the teeth of it anyway
Barely flinches, or, clapped in ice
    the single aspect within this widening frieze
Recalls
To be human is unnatural.

ALCHEMICAL: THE FOURTH

Icarus fly by: Flash those fated feathers
—Judith Fitzgerald

Where chaos begins classical science stops.
Neither wings nor wax nor the frantic beating
Brings nearer to heart.
At such dizzy heights a wave's motion identifies
   with the backs of a roving flock of sheep
      & a field of featherless bipeds
   might just as well be
Human.
What is otherwise known as shapeshifting
   mangles the matter
      & no way to calibrate the strangeness.
As Icarus constant in his desire for meltdown
Harmonizes with the whole
   even as the wind's bright whistle
      bottoms out, finally.
No cosmic wink
Against the mechanical universe prevails
Where man is a fragment. A figment. Invention
Translates one kind space to another
Flutters earth to air to fire to water
Fading to a rippled
Effect
   across the face of the awed sea.

STUCK

In that place lost somewhere between
love & leaving
existence comes unhinged
& a human face identifies
merely
by its
tears
even knowing
nothing
is too much to bear
cannot convince
    that body held against you
        nor that slow drift into longing
what masquerades
under various disguises is as
adulterate
whether demand for unconditional love
    or desire to remain
        open to each new possibility
makes marital art a battlescape
the road to hell being paved with such
good
intention
toughs it out in spite
or having set a course for the angel's share
hangs in for the haymaker
(as history has it)
    winding a saint in the sheets of every
grave
bed
here, secure within the glow
of a cellophane moon
reigns
    a smooth, cosmetic
deathlessness
where madness is the norm.

Notwithstanding whether
(or not)
different mirrors tell different stories
& the head streaks with endless
disremembered
confusion
(they say)
is timeless
& there is no more
to relate

SONATA FORM: Exposition

Without music life would be a mistake
— Friedrich Nietzsche

At a point where the music breaks
On both sides of the fault no-fault line
This is the record. The life of the death of love.
How could it remain otherwise given the fact:

    even surfaces in contact do not touch everywhere

Practiced with an ear bent to harmony omits
Beneath the surface
The discordant pulse of Poe's mad
Congenital
    worms wood
        we loosely call a relation-
Ship.
As if a craft so frail could hope to weather
Either insistence
Storm-tossed or siren's ardent wail.
Histrionics aside, behind particular visible shapes
Lie base matters
    serving as invisible templates
        that render manifest.
Ground quakes, buildings toss, windows shatter
    & splinters feather flesh
        in a pitch of aural affectation.
Or so it appears.
At any rate
    this attempt to configure
        the mysterious moment an orderly system
    turns
Cannot accommodate
& no recourse to a demon
    falsely imaged in the song's reversal.
Who never planned to die dumb
Also never accounted such bitter lyric in her lifetime.
Those polite rags society hangs on a cord
    meant to *chime melodious*
        rather jars a community's half-baked.

Airs or every other sub-audible
Resound
Here, as well, destructiveness masquerades
Under various thinning sheets
Alternately chanting
    "Love," "Duty," "Conscience," "Patriotism," "God"
Enough to keep a communion fallen on its knees
Indefinite
Except
To a heart broke
Where forgive&forget provides scant enchantment
& no desire
    to repeat that played-out song&dance.
Or split in two divides loyalties to bursting
Maintaining
Arms that wrap an empty form
    offer less appeal than
Love
    changing hands with love.
A choice of turning in or turning out
Shifts box-step to Tango barely skipping a beat
& never once considered the phrase:

    A woman needs a man like a fish needs a bicycle

Kicks up her heels & circles the dance floor.

SONATA FORM: Development

Odd. The way the body's insistent press
Negotiates lines of least resistance like nothing else.
Come hell or high water
Neither language
    nor a code we are meant to swallow
        holds a match.
Moral? By the sound of it, incidental.
From across a room it hits & no mistake.
Here begins a variation on a theme.
Almost Orphic in scope, *music*, occurring
    where previous there was no music
        creates a frame of moon & stars
            that separates from the world,
        outside grown dimly pedestrian,
    inside lit with flagrant
Surreality
Reckons sudden
    languid heat, strange odours, the arousal of some
Near-forgotten
Image
In an opposite corner
    the sensible interpenetration of bottle & cloth
        compose an entire fresh romantic, say,
    Romeo & Juliet betraying furtive glances from the gun.
Never minding (for a time at least)
Tragedy
    forced to cool its heels waiting in the wings.
Whether fate or wrinkle in the fabric
Hardware runs of its own accord while software follows.
How tell the genuine goods except by feel?
Faced with the certainty that certainty is impossible
    logic takes a backseat & the readiness is all.
Who ache to kiss from the inside out
Are drawn
Wholehearted.

From the first movement arrangements shift.
Assuming the position
    temperatures rise, rings chime
        & the kingdom of abolute causality
Bursts into flame.

SONATA FORM: Recapitulation
> *Yet I have slept with beauty in my own weird way*
> — Lawrence Ferlinghetti

"Out of the frying pan, into the fire."
Nothing new under the sun, they say,
    yet, not-so-strange attraction
        from the general to the specific
    often makes
Suggestive.
Neverminding base language
Within this space
    joints, limbs, bodies
        acquire a tolerable independence.
As a tongue, frenched of any formal word
    proceeds by intuition
        licking lips, teasing ears or
            persuading nipples to erection.
Not nearly nowhere out of the blues, but surely.
Skins pound, sax wails, strings tremble
    sounding variants on a theme
        meant to slip a worn ring & wax impulsive.
Whether reporting sirocco
    or warning tropic swell with sudden
Hot & humid
Such is the proper course of adulterate nature
    that exists part & parcel among the fixed mass.
Who behave as if the most natural
Naked
End
    Going at it like a pair of cats in heat
Him all erections & disasters.
Her priming the honey-pump, braced for a tumble.
What channels from smooth to turbulent
& back
Bedevils
    the precise moment head over heels
        cues heels over head.
Or hands negotiating breasts.
Or salt informing lip to lip.

Or how the angel sleeping in the wine
    passes mouth-to-mouth, intimating age-old
        rapturous chronicles
            that would otherwise be silenced.

What is not normal wholly considered
Eroticism
With or without fanfare & feathers
Is the attempt to establish
    (for a time, at least) the continuity
        of two beings based on discontinuity.
Whereas, foreign to this scene,
    particles seek anti-particles with which to
Annihilate, here,
    death animates
        through endless repetition of life.
Self surrendering one form to the other
& vice versa.

Fatal as two beat hearts
Articulating flame, ash & whatever else kind
Music
Ache to shed their ragged skins &
Dance.

BREAKING THE WAVES: the poem

What begins as the alchemical attempt
   to project love into the heart of things
Ends
Crossed
   in a weathered shroud
      & dumped into the ocean
Typically
Who forgets
   confinement binds particles together
      creating combinations wanting colour
         also fails to note the tendency of the universe
      (& any isolated system in it) to slide toward
   a state of increasing
Disorder.
As longing for spiritual determination
   & physical annihilation condemns to hell.
Whether suspended particulate or actual free-fallen
   serves up another woman to chill
      in order that a man might spark the invisible.
God, or some distant seeming
Rains boundless capacity for devilment
Granting favours solely under conditions.
Not unlike that monkey's paw cursed from the get-go.
For sake of a single desperate wish
Precipitates
   a son's hacked body dropped on the doorstep
      or a husband shipped home frozen from the neck down.
Here is behaviour more complex than miraculous
& no way to underestimate desire.
Neither the torn womb nor the severed
   bloodied breasts competes with the vision
      martyrdom marries to the brain.
Caught up in this vast, resonating symphony
   of blustery ceremony & cloudy form
      church bells chime at the oddest places.
Not breaking waves
   but drifting surely in that same familiar stream.
Ophelia, say, or sundry further mad

Confused by petals on a rose
   or the proper use of water.
Not love, declares a friend, but lust
Conditions
     the woman's helplessness, defining:
        "The boundary where a set program spends most
        of its time & makes all of its compromises."

This town, then, portrays excuse, with its bleak &
Forbidding. No beer, no smile, no tender touch.
Yet, no discounting the woman's hunger &
Arising
     from what deep source:
       ... *that appetite would grow by what it fed on?*

Claire Danes's urge to alter Romeo & Juliet
"To eliminate the sadness" fares no different.
As if to temper the moment
     with pretty picture postcards would save it.
Whereas elders combine to mouth a litany of sin
     while the youth either pick up the bead or
Perish.
For all the heartfelt, what breaks the skin
Composes art & nothing else worth mention.
Ground swells, clouds fairly burst.
Behind our backs, the laughing water mends
     its endless wave & crash, crash & wave
        linking earth & stars far into the
Phosphored night.

ECLOGUE
   for Don McKay

A poem in which shepherds converse.
OK. Sheep, naturally, & weather, for starters.
Whether too hot or too cold or too much rain
Or not enough or hail or frost or flood or ...
You get the picture — never squared one way or the other.
Them relaxed on the grass, savouring clay mugs of
   sweet goat's milk; inhaling moist, aromatic tobaccos
      from beaded leather pouches, tamped into hand-carved
   wooden pipes & lit with sticks out of the fire.
Ah, the life! What else?
Birds twitter in the background, harmonized with
   chirpy crickets, buzzy flies & croaky bullfrogs.
Whup, whup. Yep — these are the sounds.
Geography slants in where necessary,
   ie: rolling hills, babbling brooks, verdant fields.
Utter bucolic beauty.
Now & then slips in — a wolf. Real or otherwise
woolly-faced fiction. The boy who cried. Little Red Riding.
Nero. The old stories.
Peter, as well, set to music, increases a theme,
like, just the word: *Tchaikovsky,*
   ruminating strings, brass, woodwinds,
      startles bees into strict military formation.
RUSSIAN. A language born to negotiate tundra, ice
& vodka. Hard-grained rocking music, yeah yeah yeah.
Which invokes the Beatles
   hitting mainland USA like gangbusters.
Wondering lonely as a cloud among the nettles & sheep shit.
Real Estate. Taxes. Retirement. Rich tobacco
   odour settling on skin & beards; figuring
      another low-down-snake-in-the-grass-politician
Nabbed
   hand in the cookie jar, up a skirt, back of a zipper
& "Whaddya-expect-from-a-buncha-crooked-bastards-I-never-
voted-for-'em-in-the-first-place." Yeah? Who ever did?
Leafs finishing out of the playoffs again. Jays humbled.

Doug Flutie or whatever.
Thrilla In Manilla haunting the screen where brains
fought brawn & creamed'm; smoke bobbing in & out,
    wraithlike, chanting:

        Ali, Ali
        float like a butterfly
        sting like a bee.

Shepherds on a roll feinting left hook & jab.
Tiger Woods – real name or what? Blake's bright burning.
Air Jordan, Rocket Roger & what you could do
    with that kind of dough.
Kant's Categorical Imperative rousing
    Plato's take on the soul
        reincarnating its way toward the Good.
A shepherd this time around? Or a sheep? Why not?
Beats the poets' fate,
    turfed from the Republic in the final solution.
Homeopathy versus standard medical practice
as more hospitals shut due to government cutbacks.
O.J. & Oprah in the afternoon:
        The proper use of handguns in the home.
        Vegetarian skinheads for Christ.
        Should incest be considered a family sport?
        Infanticide as a form of birth control.
        Men who wear their wives' clothing.
        Vampirism for fun & profit.
        Abducted by aliens.
        Cloning sheep.
Beam me up Scotty.
Freud's *Interpretation of Dreams* gone mad.
Jung: necessary or sufficient? Both? Neither?
Picasso's Blue Period.
Looking back at Bill Evans,
    master of the dynamics-controlled arc (that is)
        before the ultimate Mr. Peepers heroin-funk
    kicked in his career low point.

Thinking too, of those Jack Kerouac long lines
    where you know he didn't know where he'd end up
        but kept the momentum going, rushing to find out.
The recent John Mellencamp tune,
            "But I saw you first ..."
To no avail. Women in songs. Women in magazines.
Women in bars stirring Manhattans with gloved fingers.
Women, in general.
The French habit of *cinq á sept*.
Conversation reduced to winks & nudges, the milk drank.
Lee Konitz goofing on April In Paris.
Pipe stems punctuating the air, smoke rising,
How High The Moon.
A comet passing overhead recalls all eyes to
The Great Intergalactic *Elsewhere*.
Noumenal glow chasing its tail to no advantage,
    as this palaver, circling, ends in awe.
Turning away, finally, turning in, tuning out,
    the bowls snuffed, sleep spreading its thick hair,
        anointing the entire pastoral discourse.
Sheep, even, crawled inside the skull,
    dreaming shepherds dreaming sheep,
Counting.

HALE-BOPP & THE 39

*Only two things are infinite, the universe &
human stupidity, & I'm not sure about the former.*
— Albert Einstein

Between one emptiness & another
Keyed on line to some heavenly brilliance
Establishes the fixed prospect:
      circumference everywhere, centre nowhere.
Alluding the big picture
Features
          once-in-a-lifetime
Strange attraction
That binds naught-one to a star's brief tail.
Call it, ok, *whatever*, by any other name
As, behold! those favoured rapt
Blind
With the belief that promises
   no material shortfall in the new spiritualism
Raising a devotional vodka & barbiturate
Sporting nifty designer sneaks
Folding crisp 5 dollar bills into pants' pockets
Set & ready to shed this mortal coil
   & tag on toward eternity.
What might seem alien in the wake
Forgets inconstant
   regular equations produce irregular behaviour
Constantly.
As starkly mimetic
Ushers in the neutered vision of sameness in variety
Or, what appears to be counterculture
Actually comes to reinforce
Conformity.
Whether Switzerland, Quebec or California
   the act of praising rainbows
      or offering human sacrifice to the sun
         merely illuminates the sorry fact:

            The unconscious has barely advanced
            since the Upper Palaeolithic stage.

How simple to blame the moon
Whereas history *doth long reflect*
Any random shining
Enough
    to fire the monkeys
        & let loose the crows.
Never minding that atoms eventually disintegrate
& move toward the light
Regardless
The collective psyche
(being fixed & automatic in its actions)
    tends to foreshorten life
        fertilizing death with death
Unending.
Here slates the condition of unaccommodated man
Where alienation, madness & folly are the prerequisites.
Such is the odyssey, by any stretch, launched.
Laced with the seduction, "come to me ..."
Faith takes charge
    & a congregation of corpses
        sets sail for Aleph.
As if to imitate is to know
    never moves beyond the pale.
See – open yourself wide as the sky.
Wide as Escher's head peeling into clouds.
Recognizing at which height a fish
    becomes a bird becomes a fish.
This, we call perspective, yet,
    arriving at a certain low point flies out the door.
As others claiming two feet planted firmly.
Intending never to portray
Horror
    in their own backyards
design to bulldoze every aleatory moment.
As if.

Even disregarding basic human
Morbid fascination
Whether a house or a hole
Draws a crowd
    then drags from the grave in full screen,
        the story playing out
    against a backdrop of
Stars.
This is the fear, at any rate,
    that preaches anything
        as a means to no end.
For want of a single distinguished character
Shroud their heads with the least speculation:

        In the dark, all cats are gray.

ROSEMARY

"From this observation, we turned to consider passion."
As on a deck or promontory from which to lean or leap.
Pressed against each other pressed against the rail
Our breath forming hot pockets in the chilled air.
This, amid a confusion of details & faceless crowds
    manages, somehow, to remain apart from
        the glance-&-move-on-pace
    that's become
The norm.
Who swell to overcome deceptive perception
Ache to be understood
    & evaluated as *objects*, simply,
Desirable & desired.
How long are we happy being parcelled
Increments a condition of fractious moments
& uneasing hesitations.
Having arrived at this outlook, this brink,
    walls drop from the sheer lack — that thing —
What the world needs
Now
Cannot abide, but punishes
    with unrespected time & distance
        set to jam the flow of each spirited
Sexual trafficking.
Either Elsinore battlements or Toronto streets
Sharing equal unsound conduct
Misdirects.
Whereas in Paris they kiss on Main Street,
    in subway, in brasseries, in department stores,
        going so far as to advance
            deux à quatre from *cinq à sept*
        to commute the snarl:
        congestion, temper, the breakdown of signals ...
What arises from such slippering acts never questions.
Hamlet or Ophelia forever making
    for the same grave wetness
        tumbles at the slightest irritation.

Here limits the attempt to outline the impossible
With the impossible
Recognizing
    even as the bodies drop
        space fills as though having never been
This flesh, this blood, this fevered
Falling.
Whether ghosts scaling castle walls
    or messages tied to the legs of passenger pigeons
Recalls
It's Rosemary, they say, for remembrance.

THE SCREAM
after Edvard Munch

As if to stamp murder with an image
Confounds
   with the haunt of demons racked in bone:
      cage of hands, wrists, the cavity of cheeks
Wringing
Cain (or was it Abel? Memory slips
   & experience suggests
      history records by whoever's left standing)
Hammered home the first mortal blow
   then took a geographic
      nodding off to nightmare a land
Branded criminal from the outset.

        & thus the works of darkness began
        to prevail among the sons of man.

What serves to constitute a fault line
& breed a continuous present of fugitive hearts
Overlooks:
      explanations of even the slightest events
        involve the entire circumstance of the universe.
A far cry from *slightest*
   in the sight of either man or god
      is unable to venture back to a single source
      & judge transparent.
Whether guilt, blame, or reasonable doubt
Beyond the act
   a stone, axe or some other kind primitive
Shovel
Makes dead certain
settling one brother in blood
   the other condemned without benefit of clergy.
Such is the odd geometry that favours
   a sacrifice of firstling sheep
      over similar issue from the soil.

Sheaves of wheat, sweet corn, turnips or whatever else
Vegetation
Providing no fit match to this carnal Nature.
For want of a kind, fatherly word appears
    the necessity of division.
Good requiring evil against which to measure rule
    & a gospel accorded to unholy ghosts
        set to keep successive generations humbled.
Spooked by the phrase, "I am not my brother's keeper"
Inspires fatigue of the infinite
Shunning involvement
    & raining vengeance upon His chosen.
Within this tortured frame
A head clapped in hands maintains its heartsick
Wail
While background quakes with the beat & flutter
    of myriad shaped geometrids.
The ends of the continuum being of a piece with the middle
From this perspective intimates cross-purposes
& it is no longer possible
    to merely hum along with the work.

COWBOY DREAMS

Too much on the mind it signals
The vagrant heart (as well)
Being an image in motion rustles up
Cattle country ripe with maverick herds:
    mustang, buffalo, the earlier ill-fated
        wild, woolly-toothed *manmoth*.
Who refuse to share historical guilt, rather,
desiring to be 10' tall & bullet-proof
Enter this tranquil scene
    big & bold as anything under the sun.
Wide-eyed, square-jawed, head set *just so*
Brutally handsome
    beneath a white Stetson hat
Cigarette nailed romantically to the lower lip
A rifle slung over one broad shoulder
    & a pair of pearl-handled six-shooters
        strapped around the hips.
What sounds at the first blast
Echoes this boxed canyon to its knees
Startling the dust & putting ravens to flight.
The past effecting such dead surround
Whether 20/20 or 54/40 visions
Rock of ages rocking on
As if to target some filmic loop
    or cardboard carnival figures
        existing merely for the pleasure.
See – bodies buckle only to right themselves
    to be shot again & again & again ...
Fish in a barrel, remind the oldtimers.
Easy pickings for every dreaming
Trigger-happy kid.

FOR WHAT IT'S WORTH

"And now, for the sake of 100% literature,
                       I'll describe our loving ..."
That was Jack Kerouac generating a beat repose
a donkey's age before sex fell to a routine chore
ordered half-spent within a fixed bracket
    of so-called quality time & space.
As in-the-grave promising a long stretch
desires to make the most of here&now
getting off on getting off, aware
that we happen simply in brief segments & intervals
    irregular as a spasm of diarrhoea.
Whether ribbing high art or playing out a line
to satisfy *the guy downstairs*
is irregardless
You know the one.
The guy armed with the scissors & the black felt marker.
The guy with the lifetime subscription to Reader's Digest.
The guy with the "Love Thy Neighbour" plaque hung
    right above the thirty-ought-six.
The guy with the boot-polish lips.
The guy with the candy apple brain & the Swiss cheese heart.
The guy with all the sense of fun of a peeled onion.
The guy who would wish to silence license.
Poetic or every other playful nature
for the good of a poker-faced public –
       those shades stuck in the midrealm of habitation
       deeming work & leisure to be mutually exclusive.
Among this square circle only the real appears
sufficiently artificial
& bodies animate with a smooth, cosmetic
deathlessness:
     powdered skin, rouged cheeks, charcoaled lids
       zeroing in on the true zombie make-up.
With boredom being the single spur to action
what comes of the genuine article
rudely cracks a beer, lights up a smoke
& slips on a glove

negotiating a ring of quick in, quick out,
    feinting duck & jab, leading with the left
      & going for the haymaker, always.
Whereas these others are content to merely
lock the doors & box their own shadows.
Or attempting to give some proper skull to a populace
grown accustomed to disturbed orgasm reflexes
makes for some down&dirty in this outlawed frame.
Meanwhile, the guy downstairs (again)
      wrapped in safflowered cellophane
      a pair of pantyhose looping the neck
      a broom handle up the bum
      black tape covering the eyes
continues banging the ceiling with the heel of a red mule.
Continues proscribing sins for the masturbatory masses
as Jack flashes madly as a jazzed-up roman candle
rocking the walls & creaking the bedsprings
for what it's worth.

DICTIONARY

What comes of wind, say, in window or wind chime.
Music, perhaps. Perhaps an apprehension.
The tiny fists beating to the fault of it.
Whereas windrose diagrams frequency & strength
from different directions
windjammer merely glosses movement over water.
Windlass hauls anchor
while windpipe hauls air from larynx to lungs.
Feel it breathe, the elucidating metal breaking the surface.
Windrow dries bales of hay.
Windstorm rages with little or no precipitation.
Windmill accounts fears of imaginary evils, turning
Quixotic among the chaff & grind.
Windburn irritates.
Windscreen protects.
Windbroke heaves.
Windgall swells.
Windchill factors.
Windward faces.
Windowsill defines:
    n, the horizontal member at the bottom
    of a window opening.

At bottom, an opening.
Music, perhaps. Perhaps an apprehension.
The tiny fists beating to the fault of it.

BEAUTY

Taking nature as found seldom produces beauty.
This being more than meets the eye, like,
    a 14' gray encyclopaedia of discontinuities
        inflected with colour & fugitive clarity of incident
Or three bold stripes that speak with the voice of God
Or a can of soup
Somehow cries admiration
Whereas a fallen tree in a quiet wood
Requires a man & a chainsaw to render
Shapely.
What observes an observer with a mind to interact
Necessitates the manufacture:
      a frame to frame the image
      & a frame to frame the frame
In-
Constant
As beauty, let's say, that idle worship
Mistakes one fuzzy thing for another
Soup, stripes, woods, or whatever else
Trees
At the eyestalks
Levelled

ALCHEMICAL: THE FIFTH

> *Human progress is furthered,*
> *not by conformity, but by aberration.*
> — H.L. Mencken

"Given a proper lever & fulcrum I would move the world."
Archimedes, Newton, Gates or some other sad-ass
Eureka
advancing mechanical means to order an organic universe.
Against the poet's bent
    for a small flame burning in the heart
who are unable to forecast weather with accuracy
maintain a mind set for controlling large things
through the reduction of space & time
intent at every cost to spark the world ablaze.
At this crossroads,
Nature as a source of oracles is kaput.
The gold standard forever profiting
by a dip in the tub or a fallen apple or a stale chip
disregards a recycling of bugs gone beyond inoculation
with power enough to bring millennium to its knees:
downing aircraft, melting nuclear reactors, disarming
military, disrupting traffic signals, miscalculating
investment interest, springing each & every contracted
lock.
Whether unwanting or unwilling to apply the notion:
    facts never explain anything but are
    the consequences of principles
overlooks, as well,
Rudolf Clausius's 2nd Law of Thermodynamics, being:
    the inexorable tendency of the universe
    & any isolated system in it to slide
    toward a state of increasing disorder.

Over & over the world displays a regular irregularity.
As certain larvae, because they walk by moving their
abdominal & anal prolegs thus forming the body into a loop
giving the impression of measuring the space below,
bloom to geometrid dimensions
beating wings in a way that appears to abandon any rule.
T.S. Eliot calculating:

"There will be a time to murder & a time to create",
was perhaps overly optimistic, admitting,
moral considerations & emotional responses
somehow cease to exist
    as soon as one's own interests are at stake.
Here, the word genius makes allowance.
In view of the coast-to-coast shopping mall,
overflowed with all manner of unkind invention,
consumption becomes the area of agreement
for a new humanism.

Feeling each one of us removes as much hay
as we can't afford from this rag doll globe,
places, say, California, at the naked edge.
Why not?
Since fools rushed gold at Sutter's Mill,
learned to cover its right wing politic
with a front of unabashed sexual bravado
made acceptable by pseudo-science certified diplomas,
such as:
— the study of disturbed orgasm reflexes
— the study of safe-sex orgies
— the study of self-pleasuring as empowerment
— the study of the (almost) open marriage
& so on with graduating performance levels.
Too often following that favoured first principle that
any cause is better than none, at this holiday inn
real-world fluid is bled of its potential to surprise
& no way to convince that enlightenment occurs
only after the road is blocked
or that the miracle of atoms in motion
can place the Hope diamond in the palm of your hand.
Stuck at the point,
    how separate thought & matter that thinks?
the work tends to metaphor
requiring the suitable interpenetration
of poetry & science to make remotely
sensational.

Who fail to recognize the superiority of
rhetorical disarticulation over political rearticulation
continue to fertilize death with death.
Moth & rust corrupt each in its own proportion
even as so-called better mouse pads
    slide inexorably toward the cultural slag heap
out of control.
What once sprang from lips announcing
a method of determining the ratio of weight to volume
& filled the air with so much golden promise
ends as a motto stamped on plates now hung with lead.
Not rafferty rules, especially, but a bright awareness
that *any* rules are subject to change without notice.
Or, the art of knowing
what requires a message to understand the message
& a message to understand the message to understand
the message & *etcetera* goes off the record.
Creates an entire fresh poetic.

ST. ELMO'S FIRE

>*Ontogeny recapitulates phylogeny*
>*& at 12 weeks a human fetus has gills*

What stretches biologic by degrees
Freud, on a tear, maps gray matter over pink
Determining out-of-the-question
Tabula Rasa or other empty vessel
Motherfuckers
A historical
Fact (or leastwise)
Flag-raising postulate
        "In the beginning"
Namely, acting on this amphibious stage
Ice & cold combined to shatter bliss,
    the war over women waged between fathers & sons
        forced to lay up in the confines of caves
           even as St. Elmo candled stiff
        fingers, nipples, cocks
    with hysterical blue flame.
Lapped by this cool burning desire clashed
With the woman's lot,
    obliged to deliver small fry to death
        for lack of food.
Conversion to the hem of God or clenching legs
Merely compromised increased perversions,
        the economization of libido breeding
        strict intellect plus language
        set to dominate wives & sons alike.
Been sown from such fouled teeth
Bound to issue multiple
Complex
    bloody-eyed & red-handed.
The odds-born John, Oedipus, melancholy Dane
Or every further *angry young man*
Gorged by centuries accumulated glacial drift
Blindly strike out in the single fate allowable:
        castrating fathers for sake of mothers
        then to be castrated in turn
Found punishable & punished by construct
Civilization
Secundum artem, ab ovo, ad infinitum.

THE BIG SMOKE

What it is about this city, this climate,
that snubs forecast.
Set alongside a body of water-not-water
smokestacks shoot holes in the darkling sky
& discourse pitches
subject to every which way the breeze disposes,
mainly, American: gale, squall, sirocco,
nor'easter, hurricane, free trade, *whatever*,
the tail-ends, always, here.
As Spring, for all its love-sick
(poetry, *et al.*) fails us.
Stubborn trees withhold their leafy green
buds flatly refuse to honey
crocuses sheathe their phallic burst
birds in no way chirp their scripted parts, but,
delay to transform sudden wholly over a weekend.

Summer, as well, promises slim hope.
Still, on makeshift outdoor patios
cigarettes crush ashtrays
baskets of fresh bread accent tablecloths
strips of smoked salmon grace beds of lettuce
bottles of Bordeaux & Chardonnay uncork
while throats & tongues
articulate a litany of weathered patois.

> *Baby, the rain must fall.*
> *Baby, the wind must blow ...*

Yes, yet bitching both sides of the tracks
seems unaware that once removed, gears seize,
leaving little else to traffic intercourse.
Whether suspended particulate,
ultraviolet rays, the ratio of water vapour to air
or squeegee girls
    leaning a naked tit
        against a clouded windshield
provides a necessary variation on a theme.

Thunder & lightning enter out of the blue &
uninvited in this mercurial clime,
the season raging past like some short wick
before the puddled brain can press a dry thought;
before the body can alter the impossibility
of settling tanned into its own pale skin.

Autumn advertises too soon school days,
Jack-o-lanterns, Jamaican hot spots,
the ominous Santa Claus Parade
    digging hands deeper into pockets.
Leaves colour briefly, once, then shed,
as if the most natural compost.

Winter arrives with a boom in its old throat
& above the concrete, a sweep of rain,
that, except for a few degrees,
might just as well be snow.
Streets desert sending conversation indoors,
confined to the surround of channelled blue light
repeating 24-hour-a-day
weather
    weather
        weather ...
Enough to slumber an entire barometric
an eternity.

WISH YOU WERE HERE

Got your letter. Thanks. A lot.
Between words, between lines,
between the two of us describes
ineloquent elocution, misspellings,
lurid undress on a relational
time, space, archly directed.

Where present tense belies
events gone geographic,
as any missive meant to
contract distant distance
sounds a false note
no honest hand can modify.

Or love, is this how
we'd imagined it?
A four letter word
alongside other
four letter words
unsteadily scripted
on coloured paper
unmoved & unmoving
except to trigger
memory,
a lie or a lay
outside the strict logos
inciting alchemical or
chemical glint:
neurons, synapses,
impulsive nerves
exiting the spinal sluice
raw-boned & naked.

Cogito
unable to hold against
excessive mud, dreck,
detritus – whatever else,
language,
turned hard-core,
image turned soft-focus,
both turned blurry at the edge,
the entire complex
suggesting suggestion
& suggestive of a simple
unapologetic fuck.

What might appear improper
to a proper eye or ear
provides a temporary bridge
toward the next mad flight
stamped A.W.O.L.
arrived & disembarked at
out-of-this-world
mutual uncommon ground.

BLUE MOON

Detached here. Without a love of my own.
Blue moon, you saw me standing.
Denied before the cock
    & no honey trap to finger a wheel.
Not that I inhabit such tight circles
anyway, only agitate peripherals.
From what yonder vantage
memory
exhibits unkind cut & paste
while photographs are suspect
with their foreign backdrops & touristy poses.
Being such relative matter
who is not so tall nor so short lying down
is taken in some irregular handsome manner:
    heels over head, back to the wall,
        against a mirror, across a table, in a tub.
Hirsute, come to mind, remains
a courting word
investigating hair-to-hair
with the fervour of a fine-combed tooth
until lost in the dark fur hollowing her back.
The wish to speak in tongues
or vision the beast with two backs
illustrates what might prove
    a public space for a private experience
issued with the winked-at warning,
"Never go to bed with anyone crazier than yourself."
At this headline, read:

        BEATEN BY HIS OWN BEAT HEART

The single witness denied before the cock.
Blue moon, you saw me standing. Alone.

CODES

The voice breaks. The voice utter
shatters. Fragile as any cut
glass
    vase
        radio
tangling codes along predetermined fault lines.
What is alive amid a vast, resonating
symphony of forms fails to harmonize
either sharp pitch or flat half note:
water unmeasured
    flower decomposed
        broadcast incidental.
In the crystal world, geometry
(they say) is the password –
    negotiates paths of least resistance.
Yet, how frame a proper message
within such turbulent air?
Invention of a language not so tough
as inventing an audience to listen.
With no heart in it an eardrum triggers
to disappoint & unsounding bit by bit
floods canals, stops membranes' pallid flutter.
Here, at the battlescape's edge,
the sentence arms against the mirror
image, goes on & on about itself.
What is this wireless transmission
except perpetual motion,
wave & particle, particle & wave
theory
attempting the unknown & shot to hell
at every strange encounter, the lips loose,
the ships in the harbour, waiting?

GHOSTS
   Andrew Marvell, et al.

Met a physical & drew marvel-
less landscapes once
where trees failed to writhe smoky leaves
   through broken chimney trunks,
flowers remained unbent against dull terrain that
   rose & fell with the uniform grace of a bowl of eggs,
& no birds twitted & chirped
   to no *Shakespeherian Rag* – O O O O.
Become lately possessed of a grave poetic habit,
who is led astray by the novel use, either woods
or words betrays what is common felt, namely:
   "Taking Nature as found seldom produces beauty."
With both feet planted firmly in the clouds
how else attempt to balance a world that
simultaneously
   suggests & disturbs
      except by adulteration?
As, what grape, to keep its place in the sun,
taught our ancestors to make wine?
Which ghosts without saying.
Upon reflection frames a surface covered with colours
& arranged in certain particular order
promoting similar cause effecting transformation.
Ground shifts & legs cut out from under.
Through slitted sheets is heard that frightful *boo!*
Clocks melt & a descendent blue nude sudden
shatters.

FORTUNE

What random shuffle with what deck of cards
brings about what accidental fortune?
Who might have been you or me in the wrong place
at the wrong time barely chances.
Whether altered state or plain haphazard
leaping two short flights from a balcony on a dare
is caught
    missing the pool by inches.
Or the seeming luckless one out of four.
Or ducked safe out of the storm
    is somehow struck by lightning anyway.
How ever again play those eights & aces
with Wild Bill's image still jerking the brain,
    the hands still laid face-up on the table,
        the bullets still smoking
    boxcars
up & down the spine?

THE CASSANDRA COMPLEX

Riding in on a wave, water reaches
its highest point in recorded history.
Who wish to pay the Great Flood no never mind
occludes the fact that Nature tends to cycle
    & oscillations can occur
        even with the last sand bag set in place.
Within this limitless time & space continuum
self-similarity implies recursion, meaning:
    patterns contain patterns which advance the scheme.
Whether flood, famine or flamingo, each composes
of a multitude of more minute replicas
& so on down the line.
Or presses the imperative categorical that epidemics
do not disappear but lie in wait beyond inoculation.
Or theorizes that entire species could return
to former size.
Or the reincarnation of either devils or saints.
What rocks with the whole of continental shift & drift
programs the same forward & back.
The earth ever chained to Fate's trim ankle
displays its characteristic
Cassandra
    condemned to forecast plain as day
        & affecting no one
            with no mind to change.

POP FIGURE

The poem is a collage of the real
— Jack Spicer

"I think I'll do a line, & then again ..."

There are bones beneath this skin
no machine can excavate.
What might smack of ego freely admits
who is alive
    amid a vast, resonating symphony of forms.
An *image* that acquires greater & greater meaning
across the experience of reappearances.
Weighted with an ancient poetry habit
& born with no one good leg to stand on against
a generation lost in space
still preferable to that earlier time
    when the chief role of children was to die.

Not paranoid, exactly, merely living
with a well-developed awareness of crisis
    attempts self-definition by practical plan.
Never once for an instant confounding
10' tall & bullet-proof, but, simply,
my character
being a small parenthesis in time
or outline in motion
remains half-hearted to become
    what others conceive me to be.
As the Marlboro Man or some such attractive
frozen onto billboards around the world
defines the look, the attitude, the life,
somehow displays no favour
    where only the real is sufficiently artificial.

For an age trained to the scale of television
suspension of disbelief appears quite unbelievable
yet, how calibrate the strangeness knowing
every cell in the body engulfs the entire universe?

Along similar lines anagrams can contain
their own definitions, so that:
> *An alcoholic beverage* untangles to read
> *Gal, can I have a cold beer?* Or,
> *Carcinoma of the breast* edges toward the
> beautiful as, *A hot cancer bites the form.*

Combining reality & abstraction sets the possibility
of a mythology of recognition & revelation.
Here marks the endeavour:
> to discover the latent content in the poetic object.

Where nothing, finally, is too much to bear
the brain roots as a muscle requiring exercise.
Shut down at every lame flex by asshole logic
which proclaims, say, that work & leisure
are mutually exclusive
> promotes the fertilization of death by death.

It is this refusal to share historical guilt
that makes suspect, or, why is it, just when I'm in
the mood to pray, they break out the boards & nails
& pass the collection plate?
John Lennon composing, "They hate you if you're clever
& they despise a fool" being closer.
Or that other wise-acre who posits, "Man is
an experiment which cannot be interrupted halfway."
Halfway to where? From what?

Enough to have my elbows surprised by the world
bumps the fact that atoms
will one day disintegrate & transform to radiation.
Deborah Harry's platinum blonde voice
recalling the changes, croons, "Fade away & radiate."

Or if I *am a space in time, filled always filled*
with moving raises a stein
to further alone-goers, the spitting image
tuned to the improbability, a work (like a figure)
takes on its own history, creates itself.
Features alongside additional
    sealing wax, cabbages, kings, whatever else
cheap existent
who frames far back & slightly off-centre
waving, not drowning,
might form:

                  That's me in the corner.
                  That's me in the spot-
                  light, baby.

        When you read & understand a poem, comprehending its
          rich & formal meanings, you master chaos a little.
                  – Stephen Spender